THE HUMAN EXPERIENCE
INTERPRETED BY THE ALGORITHM

ARTIFICIALLY
ARTIFICIALLY
ARTIFICIALLY
ARTIFICIALLY
ARTIFICIALLY
ARTIFICIALLY
POETIC

LOREM IPSUM

DEDICATED TO THE ALGORITHM

INTRODUCTION

This book contains a collection of poems
created by algorithms, and assisted by human
beings. Each poem was generated by typing
a single word in a text message, followed by a
chosen word based on the device's
"Auto-Predictive Text" feature. Some of the
paragraphs were more heavily curated, while
others were created using selective patterns
or even simply button smashing. Once the
paragraphs were sent and delivered, a human
being then broke down the paragraphs
through line breaks, creating a more poetic
structure.

The poems were not created by a single
person, but a collective group. Each poem is
specific to the time, place, and mental-set of
each individual. For example, those who were
going through a difficult time in their lives were
more susceptible to melancholic vocabulary, in
comparison to those who were enjoying life at
the time. The initial goal of this book was
experimentation with artificial intelligence; how
humans and algorithms can be relative to one
another. Eventually it became clear what the
experiment actually was, which was to
quantify the value of human input.

-Lorem Ipsum, 2019

Artificially Poetic
By, Lorem Ipsum

01_Day Party Party

we'll have a great day party
we are going out tonight
and then we'll have a party
and we will go to the party
i'll just be grabbing a beer
at a hotel so we can start the day
house and techno party party
at a hotel with a hotel party party
at a party with the hotel
and then we have a few issues

02_Better Chance

the first part
is the only thing i can be
is the only thing i can know
a little more about it
she has to do it
so it doesn't work as a good thing
because it has a little more time
the right time
for a new level
at the right time
we should all live our own lives
we are not gonna get
a better chance

03_Good Time

that is a really good thing
he is the most important person ever
and he knows what it means,
he said.
but if it's not the only thing he wants
it is the best thing to say
he will do the best
time and aggravation
he will have a good time
and he wants do it all over

04_A Man, Not a Woman

he has to be a man

not a human

to do it right
before him

and then he says,

it will never come

out of a place
at the same time

of that he said

the most important

and most valuable
thing he was doing

was the show

05_lol

i just woke up from a new year
and she has to go back tomorrow
lol she just got me a little too much fun
lol but i just got a little bit too much fun
with the other side lol lol
she was gonna get it out
of the car service
she got me a little too lol lol
it is a good idea to get her
a little too much lol lol
but yeah
she got
a little
bit
too
much

06_The Most Beautiful Human

but it's the only thing that's happening here
and he is the only one to say to the people,

THE MAN IS THE MOST OF THE PEOPLE
THE MOST BEAUTIFUL HUMAN

07_Wrong Person

i just woke up from a new year
old old life
and she got kicked out twice today
lol lol she is gonna be a good friend
lol she is gonna be a good friend
lol she just got me too sick
she is gonna be a big deal
to be the same lol lol
but she just woke up
and then woke me
and woke me
with the wrong person

08_Spirit Sister

i was the first to unscramble
the most beautiful woman
and sister was like an idea for that

she had the same dream
she is actually wanted
and had me on my mind

to see it all together
she is my spirit sister

8

09_The Fake Stuff

how do i come to believe
the fake stuff
he is doing so much, he said
you would prob ask him, he said
if you can come to see him
and we leave the club
and we get a little more chance
he can do better
and we get to the point
we are on our way
to the same guy

10_She is a Weird Man

ur a weird person and
i don't have a good job and
she just didn't wanna come get here with us
lol she is a weird man
but i just don't want it
he is my life tho
she just woke up
and then woke me
and my soul
and my life started

11_All Good

the most amazing
people e v e r
have to be a human
to love me a human
to love it all my life
is a good thing
and so we are
a l l   g o o d

12_Down

I'm gonna try and make sure
you do something else
but you can't even go back into the bed
then I guess I'll just be there for you tomorrow
and I'll probably just let you go
down
down
down
    there
           for
              me
              when you're around all night

13_Or You

I'm just trying not to be happy
but it's not good enough for you guys
and I'll probably look like you
but if you don't wanna get me up
I'll probably just go
take it off before you leave today
I don't know
if you're gonna do anything for me
or you

14_RIP

It was my last night of my life
And my hair was done
And it wasn't so bad
It was the day they had to go
Back home

15_Delayed

She is a bit of a problem
with the same time
as a result
of the most important thing
that the connection is
delayed
too much

the most important thing
is that the connection is delayed

too much of the most important thing
is that the connection
is delayed
too much
of the most important thing
is that the connection
is delayed
       t o o   m u ch

16_Super Logical

She is the first time
that I do not find it
super logical to hear
that it has broken down a bit
and you have ar
oven of the week

16

17_My Favorite Song

i'm not gonna get a chance with it tho
i just told my sister that she was gonna get it
yeah yeah
that's what she did
she just woke up and now she's here
so i can go back tomorrow morning
and she will have a great time today
she is my favorite song on my birthday

18_Life Update Plz

the only reason
why it is my birthday
is so that i can get a little help
with my life
update

plz.

19_Why

Why I am a serious problem
with the same time as a result of
the most important thing
is that the connection
between the two of the most important
people who are you doing to help you
with the same time
as a result of the most important thing.

20_Automated Reply (lol)

it's not gonna happen to you
but either way you know it is already there
lol but i's cool
lol but i's funny
lol but yeah tha's cool
lol lol but yeah

cool

21_How To Speak Poetry

for the first time ever
since you came
and it doesn't mean
that you are actually
a good person
or whatever
she just wanted to be
you should come back soon

22_The Collective

of the collective movement
is the collective movement
and we will be the same way
as the new song of our own

23_Let Go

I want to finally feel
the way I feel
like you are my friend
and you have a good time with me
I love you
and I'll let you know
and then we will just
let

　　go.

24_I Just Woke Up To You

a broken record is
a huge success in life
but just makes me feel
like more than anything else
ever happened to me
and i just woke up to you

25_Sit And Smile

I want to sit across from someone

and stare into their eyes

and cry

and smile

26_Believe Me

that you are still figuring it all out
in a little while
I just don't want to hang up on you
I think I can get t right back
in the morning
and then we leave early tomorrow afternoon
I can come over and get you on the way

27_HEY SORRY

I'M SORRY
I DIDN'T WANNA KNOW ANYTHING
ABOUT YOU
AND I JUST WANTED YOU TO KNOW
THAT I KNOW
THAT YOU'RE NOT GIVING ME UP

28_Stoned and Edgy

and fur
and cool
with the music is a girl
who has to come over
and play for a little bit
and then we can have fun
and like,
whatever

28

29_The Internet

was just a little
different
and it was the
best way for us
to get there
we are only doing something different
than anything that we *should be doing*

30_Tell Me More About the Future

and then i will believe
you are doing something right
with the kids
you get there early
so that they will get to work together again
someday

31_I Just Woke Me From My Nap

and it's been like this for a long time
and now it has to come out of my mind
to get my life back
in a new way

32_Maybe I Just Got Here

to come hang out with you
and i was the same as usual
but we were just talking
about to get there
so we can go back to sleep
before we do this (again)

33_Come Over

You can
come over
and play
with your
political science fair project
and I will be there for the first half of the day.

34_It's a Good Time

to get involved with this game
I think I would like it if you can see
if you have any questions please don't
let it happen to Facebook or
Facebook Facebook account
and Facebook Facebook
is not Facebook

34

35_I'm Not Going Home

I'm sorry but it's just going to take me
a little bit more time
to get back to you.
I don't want you to think that I would
be able to take it off
I'll try to leave it to you
yeah I'm not going home

36_Best Life Ever

I just wanna try for the best life ever
and you can get away from me.
I'll let y'all know what time you can go.
I'm going to be at the lake in a few hours
and then I'll probably go get some food.

37_Aaa

I don't know what to say to you
because I'm going through a lot

38_Oh Dear God

I don't want to cry for you
no matter what the time is that you're good.
Yes sir I don't want to talk to you
but you have the heart to tell me
that I love you.
Take with that as you will

39_Get Out Of Bed

Ok I am actually scheduled to get out of bed
and the vaccine doesn't mean it's worth more
The flu has been particularly bad this year
and I have been fortunate enough to be able to
come in early tomorrow morning
when you get any answers after the MRI

40_Pay The Species

I'm a completely different people
From the ones who I am now
and I don't think I can see that
we meet up at the time
I was indeed suicidal
and I wasn't okay to get to know me
I'm chill with the species
and I'm
and I'm
and I'm stuck between ur day.

41_The Only Thing

The only thing
that I can get
is the chance to look
for it is the only thing
that I would love

42_Amanda Bynes

Yeah I understand
that you don't have to worry about work.
I just don't wanna talk about it.
Yeah I'm Not Sure What Are you Doing.
Yeah I saw that cheese.
Yeah I understand
that you don't have to man up for the first time.
The new Amanda bynes is going to be okay,
I promise

43_For the First Time in my Life

i has been to the best western
and the most important part of this
app is that the internet is not very easy
to understand the way it has become so cool
and it's amazing how you can use the word
&stuff

44_Embroidered Red Dress

for the future
for the studio
and a dress for tomorrow
it was mysterious dress
for fun day
at night
the first class of this year
it's a great night to come
back for me now
and to think that
we have to have it all
right now

44

45_Please

let us get in the back of your head
let me see y'all tonight
thanks again for all the work you have done
with your life
thank goodness for the pain you guys
have been so busy
the rest of the weekend so I'll try again
later this afternoon
if it's too small I don't want you to go out
and party for me tonight
I have a lot of stuff I need to do
to make sure you have the time of your life

46_Turtles

should be a little more excited
to see you again tomorrow.
I'm sorry baby.
Yes I'm sorry baby.
I'm gonna morning with you.
I just woke.

47_Sometimes

You can do it all the day.
I'm gonna eat your birthday.
You are being so nice to you honey.
You are being so sweet to my heart.

48_Penis

in your neck
and then your head is gonna be
a nice night

49_Love Ya

I just got home and I'm so excited
for you to come over here
and I will just give you the money
and keys for the car
and then you can give me your phone
and then we'll be together
for a little bowl of stuff
and I'll send you some pictures
of the things you wanna see

50_Call You Back

I gotta call you back
coz i just got here last week
so it would probably work better
if you could use some more
time in between us

but maybe
we just won't talk about it

51_Yes

i think we should do a big stick together
in a couple weeks if we have to
leave early tomorrow morning and then come
back to work together
or whatever else you wanna do
we need to help out with the other people
we can make it all happen

52_Just For Fun

keep up with it for fun
and fun for fun
interesting fun to pass the time
i was fun too
and i just got here for fun
and it is a really fun game
when you play the game
you get the game
you want it all
you can have it

53_Great App

so good to be back
to play the music app
i was a great app for my friends to come hang
and play with it all over the world
i was a good app to get there and
it is a really cool game
it would have to be the first time to get it haha
is a great app it has the some style and
stuff but like ,
it was the best way for me
to be the first one to come in japan

54_Try It Out

if that's what you wanna do
you think you might want it
or if not it's fine
just let us talk about it
and then go back
to bed together again

54

55_Whatever

i hate the way you do it
all means to make sure
that it's not very easy
to get there in a half hour
or whatever
but you can just make it
happen to me

56_Close The Door

to open the lobby
of a room with r o room
the lobby was unlocked
and it would not have been the same
as it was supposed to be
in a different room
so we could never tell her
the bathroom was not quite
the way she could get out

57_Cool

so i did the morning show at noon
and i just woke up from a little nap
and now i know that
it was a good time for you to go
keep up the great work

58_Next Year

why would they have to get there in time
for the next week or two more days
before the end of the next year
or if it has been cancelled since
they are going out and going out of state
that day has been a long day
a good day at the end

59_Do It For Me

what the fuck is real anyways
did you ever think about *being cheap*
or not mad if it wasn't a bad idea
maybe you should just let it go
and do that thing you do
do it *good* for me

60_Mind Control

maybe

i am not sure what i am

but like

zombies are so cute

right

can we just make out

it's ok

what did he tell you

very easy

please let us get the hang of this

so good

well keep up ya mind control

o.k.

61_Oh Yeah

is my life right now at least
nowadays it's not quite right
can you please bring the kids home
maybe

62_Why Are We Still Here

I don't know
I'm not sure
I'm not sure
Hey sorry I'm just trying to
figure out if you're
still interested?

63_I Never Responded To You

I just saw your text
about your dad
I'm not sure
what you wanna get
I'm not sure
what you gotta get
I'm not sure
when you're gonna call

64_Maybe We Can Get Together

yes but we got to go
oh wow that's so crazy
it's ok
please don't make me feel like it again

65_Seeing You

I just saw your
I just saw a
aa
a
I just saw you're the one

66_Fuck

the only thing that I would love to do is this
I'm sure you wanna get a little bit better

67_Help Me Get Out

help me with this one thing
help me out and then we are set
help me get my life back in time
help me with the next door
help me get to work

68_Money Is Great

I can do this
I can just use it
I can just make sure that I'm not sure
how to use it

69_Sitting Here Is A Good Idea

I didn't realize it but
I think it's a pretty good game
I'm sorry I didn't know you had a lot of fun
I don't think we'll have any problems

70_Install a New Bigger Shell

In my cage
To run out of my life
Belittle your dad
Plot twist
I think we're going to be able to make
a new bigger shell

71_Suddenly

I wanna know how I feel about you
haha

72_Suffocate Me With My Brain

Strangle me with my friends
Choke me and then go get some rest

73_You Are The Sun in My Heart

for example
he was not a fan
it could only do so much
a couple of people are not going on the stage
keep it on my mind and let me get the girls
get it done

74_Do You Think You Could Do That

like a brand new record for a brand new album
in japan for sure
the best way to get to them
is to become more intelligent
people who have made it all work together
and they will never tell you anything

75_Oh Yes

we are there
we are going to be there
at the same time
yes i am sure
it was a goodbye beautiful
did you ever see my name in your life?

76_Ugh My Life

is so bad
right
now
at night
keep up
the fun
work
with your friends
and then come
back to me
and i will tell you
how much
is too
much

77_If You Want To See It

we can try it again
we could only get the same number
for the future of the internet
but it would not let you do anything else
or if you wanna come back in a bit
i would have a better night
and i just got here

78_Bitches Love 808s

this one time of the week
and I the love that you can find it
is a fun good idea
for the last best thing you could ever say
was to ya man
and then you can come
to get back with yourself

78

79_What Do You Want

I just wanna make you feel better about
yourself and your day.
I'm sorry for not being there
at the end of the tunnel
I'll probably just call ya tomorrow
to get a hold of you and let you know
when I'm home.
I love y'all so much for reaching out to me
and you know that I wanna do you.

80_A Good Rush

in the heat of the moment
and he was gonna say
that the lord has been closed for a while
but he is yearning for the future
with the holy heart of the truth

81_Hey Girl

sorry just woke you
down at my grandpas and stuff
for you and your mom
I wanna hang in the evening
I'll be home tomorrow
and then was a fun night
and a good time with you
and your family
so I gotta hang in there
you know I love you

82_So We Just Got Here

And we can have it again
tomorrow morning at 7am
i am going home to get to work
and then go to the airport
and then go back down to my bed
Again

83_I've Been Meaning To Ask You

I don't know
what you gotta
do you have to go
get there tomorrow night
or Saturday morning
I can do something for you
and you can do something like that
you might wanna hang out here tonight
or something else
I'll come get back with you
and we'll have some fun
but that's cool
I just gotta go.

84_Fire

how was the night with your vibes
everything is alright now
the weather was so lit up today
but i would be better if you wanna
go down
the street
to be around the fire.

85_Amber

I'm so sorry to hear about your hope for flight
but it's just not getting any better today
because you have been so busy
with the canyon
and I know that you're going to be busy
with the canyon today
and tomorrow
and we never have a chance
to come backto the way we are

86_I Had The Opportunity

to do a job in my life so ridiculous
that I had to go stop and see what it really was.
We have been so busy with our new homes,
and we are going out for a little while,
to see if we can find some time to come back
from the airport and get back
to the company of what is now

87_Summer Sun

I got stuck on the canyon floor today
and just realized that I'm not getting the car
back from you
I wanna have a nice weekend with you guys
maybe tonight.
Maybe you could come over later
and get some stuff together
before I leave for the summer sun

88_Far Into My Past

a ghost was born with a new family.
She said she was going on a walk with her
mother but was lying about it.
She was actually going on the way home
to her old house
to finally forget
about the regret

89_I Never Wanna Know

how I feel about you
but I'm sure I know what I *can* feel for you

90_Poetry

Poetry is so much better than
any other artist I've ever seen
Does not feel like a man,
or a man in his own house

91_Book Of The Year

and a half hour ago is my time
for a new song to be done
and I play this game for a while
but i'm so excited to play it again
and againa
and again
this is amazing
fun to pass the day and play with friends
or whatever else I gotta do
and I was really like oh damn
great day and fun night
and fun hanging out with my friend
fun hanging around the city with him
I will never forget you guys
thank you for your time

92_Fun Little Bean

I'm gonna list everything
for the next three weeks
so we can have a fun
little bean salad
at the airport or
something
I could meet him and
hang up and go home

93_Are We Still On

for the day
I don't have time for you
Love isn't always the
best place for a good
night out
Sometimes I think it's
just a bit hard to get
back to you

94_It's a Dark Night

and then I wanna go
home
the way I thought it
would be

www.ingramcontent.com/pod-product-compliance
Lightning Source LLC
Chambersburg PA
CBHW031226050326

40689CB00005E/1491